How to Tie A Sarong

C. C. Mackay

Copyright © 2011 Learn and Do

www.LearnAndDo.com

All rights reserved.

CONTENTS

[1 INTRODUCTION .... 1](#)

[2 STYLE ONE .... 2](#)

[3 STYLE TWO .... 4](#)

[4 STYLE THREE .... 6](#)

[5 STYLE FOUR .... 8](#)

[6 STYLE FIVE .... 10](#)

[7 STYLE SIX .... 12](#)

[8 STYLE SEVEN .... 14](#)

[9 STYLE EIGHT .... 16](#)

[10 STYLE NINE .... 18](#)

[11 STYLE TEN .... 20](#)

[12 STYLE ELEVEN .... 22](#)

[13 STYLE TWELVE .... 24](#)

[14 TIPS .... 27](#)

[**15 MAKING AN EASY WRAP SKIRT FOR THE BEACH OR POOLSIDE .... 28**](#)

1 Introduction

There are many ways to tie a sarong. Some are easier to wear than others. I have several sarongs and they are all different sizes. Although I've read that they are usually 2 yards by 1 yard none of mine actually measure to this size.

Also the range of styles you can tie from your sarong will depend on the size of your body. I am 5 foot 8 inches and reasonably sized. Therefore I will not be able to wrap a particular sarong around my body in the same styles as someone who is 5 foot tall and very slender.

This book has a range of tying options. Some you will be able to use and some may not suit the sarong that you are using. However by looking at the different ways you can tie a sarong I am sure that you will find styles that will suit your sarong and your body. You will be able to adapt some of the styles to your own requirements.

The second section of the book is about how you can sew a simple wrap skirt that will be useful for both beach and poolside use. If you have done any basic sewing you should be able to make it.

The starting point for the skirt is a simple skirt pattern that, if you have done any sewing, you will probably have already. The skirt pattern is used to ensure that the darts are in the proper place in the wrap skirt.

2 Style One

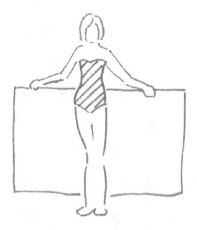

Start with the sarong held to your back with the long side held horizontally.

Take one corner to the back and over your shoulder, wrap around the body so that the other corner is to the front.

How to Tie a Sarong

Tie at the shoulder.

Variation

Tie again at the waist or hip. Choose the final length you want and tie to give you this length, this will produce a blouson effect.

3 Style Two

Start with the sarong held to your back with the long side held horizontally.

Wrap the sarong around your body, underneath your arms.

How to Tie a Sarong

Tie in the front.

Take the ends over the bust-line to the back and tie

4 Style Three

Start with the sarong held to your back with the long side held horizontally.

Wrap the sarong around your body underneath your arms and cross over at the front.

How to Tie a Sarong

Twist the corners to make them easier to tie.

Tie at the back of your neck.

5 Style Four

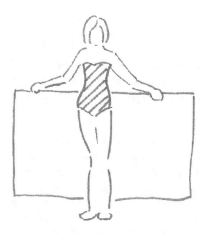

Start with the sarong held to your back with the long side held horizontally.

Tie around your waist using either a knot or bow.

How to Tie a Sarong

The tie can be either at the front or at your side.

6 Style Five

Start with the sarong held to your back, either with the long side held horizontally or vertically depending on your sarong.

Tie around the waist

How to Tie a Sarong

Take the other end of the sarong up and tie underneath your arms.

7 Style Six

Start with the sarong held to your back with the long side held horizontally.

Wrap around the waist as shown.

How to Tie a Sarong

Twist corners to make them easier to tie.

Tie at the waist.

8 Style Seven

Start with the sarong held to your back with the long side held horizontally.

Wrap around your body.

How to Tie a Sarong

Tie under your arm at one side.

Tie again at the waist or hip. Choose the final length you want and tie to give you this length, this will produce a blouson effect.

Variation

Try tying this style using the sarong vertically for a longer length look.

9 Style Eight

Start with the sarong held vertically to the front, with the short end of the sarong horizontal to the floor. Tie behind your neck.

Push sarong between your legs and hold the corners at the rear.

How to Tie a Sarong

Take the corners to the front and tie at the waist. You can roll up any extra length at the back before tying the corners at the front.

10 Style Nine

Start with the sarong held vertically to the front, with the short end of the sarong horizontal to the floor. Tie behind your neck.

Take one side around your back and tie at the other side as shown.

Variation

Choose the final length you want and tie to give you this length, this will produce a blouson effect at the waistline.

11 Style Ten

Start with the sarong held to your front with the long side held horizontally.

Take one corner to your shoulder at the rear, wrap the sarong around your body and finish with the other corner at the front.

How to Tie a Sarong

Tie over your shoulder.

12 Style Eleven

Start with the sarong held to your back with the long side held horizontally.

Tie at the front.

How to Tie a Sarong

Take the sarong from the rear between the legs and pull this up behind the knot at your waist.

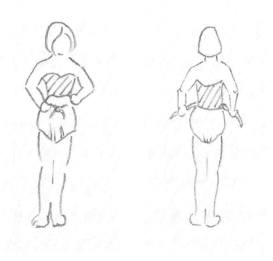

You can tie this into the knot as well.
Or take the ends around to the back and tie them there.

13 Style Twelve

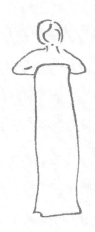

Start with the sarong held vertically to the front, with the short end of the sarong horizontal to the floor. Tie behind your back.

Push sarong between your legs to the back and hold the corners at the rear.

How to Tie a Sarong

Take the corners to the front and tie at the waist. You can roll up any extra length at the back before tying the corners at the front.

Variation

Start with the sarong held vertically to the back, with the short end of the sarong horizontal to the floor. Tie over your bust-line.

Pull sarong between your legs to the front and hold the corners at the front.

Take the corners to the back and tie at the waist. You can roll up any extra length at the front before tying the corners at the back for a tidier look..

14 Tips

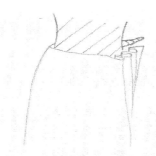

1. Pleat the fabric before tying for a smoother, draped look.

2. Your sarong can be used as a shawl for cooler evenings or for air conditioned areas that can feel a bit cold.

3. A sarong can make a handy cushion when sitting on leather or vinyl seating so that the backs of your legs don't 'stick' to the chair.

Top Tip
You can fold the sarong along the length before tying to alter the final style.

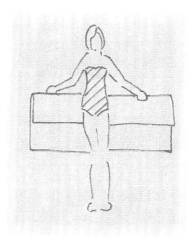

15 Making an EASY wrap skirt for the beach or poolside

This section is an overview on how to make a wrap skirt that will be very handy for beach or poolside use. I find it very convenient and comfortable to wear.

This wrap skirt has 2 front sections that overlap and an extended waistband to tie the skirt in place.

If you've done some sewing you will probably be able to make your own wrap skirt. You need a basic skirt pattern and some material.

To Start

You need a basic skirt pattern, it is really just the waistline and the position of the darts that you need from the pattern. If you have a dress pattern that has a seam at the waist it would probably work too.

Get some paper, newspaper will do, and make a copy of the back skirt pattern and 2 copies of the front skirt pattern.

Lay your copies out with the front patterns in line with the side seams of the back pattern as shown.

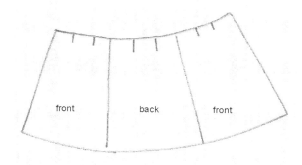

Measure the length at the waist and that is the length of fabric you will need.

Waistband

The waistband will be twice the length that you have just measured. The extra length ensures that it can be comfortably tied when worn.

Choosing material

Be sure that the width of the fabric you buy is deep enough for the length of the skirt PLUS 2 widths of waistband too. The waistband is about 1½ inches wide. So that would be the length of the skirt + three inches for the width of the 2 waistband sections.

Length of material = waist measurement from 3 patterns pieces
Width of material = length of skirt plus 3 inches

An alternative waistband could be make using tape or ribbon instead of the material.

To Make the Skirt

Once you have your material then place on the pattern pieces and mark where the darts are. Ignore the side seams and seam allowances. The final skirt will be tied to fit.

Also mark where the right hand side seam would be. This is where you will make a buttonhole. The waistband will go through this buttonhole when the skirt is tied to keep the sections in line.

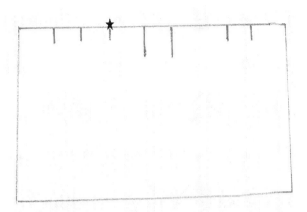

This diagram shows how the material is laid out. The darts are placed and the star is marking the side seam for the position of the buttonhole

To make it up

Sew the darts and finish off the other 3 sides of the fabric. Not the waistline edge as it will be enclosed with the waistband.

Stitch the short ends of the waistband together to give one long strip of fabric. Place this seam at the center-back.

Stitch the waistband onto the waistline of the skirt, turn the waistband to enclose the raw waist edge and stitch, enclosing all the raw edges.

Tidy the end of the waistband so that its width matches the section on the skirt.

Make a buttonhole (at the right hand side seam area of the original pattern that is shown by the star in the sketch). The buttonhole in made on the waistband and needs to be big enough for the waistband end to be threaded through it comfortably.

My wrap skirt is made in a light cotton fabric.

To wear

Place the skirt centrally at your back. Take the tie on the left hand front section and thread it through the buttonhole.

Cross the right hand section over and tie the waistband ends, with a bow, to the back or side.

Personalize it too

This is a good chance to use the embroidery stitches that you have on your sewing machine, but probably rarely use.

You could also add fringing, beads, etc. Anything that takes your fancy. You can really use your imagination for this.

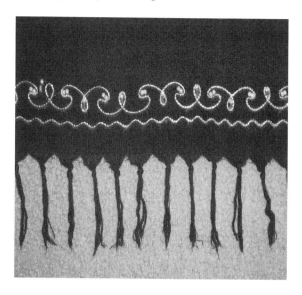

Use colors that will coordinate with your swimwear for an expensive look.

Made in the USA
Lexington, KY
05 December 2014